HOW THINGS WORK

ASTONISHING
AIRCRAFT

p

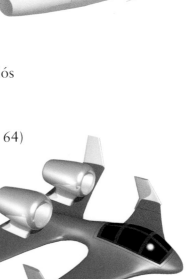

This is a Parragon Book
This edition published in 2001

Parragon
Queen Street House
4 Queen Street
Bath BA1 1HE, UK

Copyright © Parragon 2000

ISBN 0-75255-296-1

Printed in Dubai, U.A.E.

Produced by
Monkey Puzzle Media Ltd
Gissing's Farm
Fressingfield
Suffolk IP21 5SH
UK

Illustrations: Alex Pang
Designer: Tim Mayer
Cover design: David West Children's Books
Editor: Linda Sonntag
Editorial assistance: Lynda Lines and Jenny Siklós
Indexer: Caroline Hamilton
Project manager: Katie Orchard

Photos by Roger Buckingham (5, 23, 27, 29, 33, 64)
and MPM Images.

CONTENTS

WRIGHT FLYER

Propellers
The two rear-mounted wooden propellers turned in opposite directions, to make sure that the forces pushing the *Flyer* forwards were balanced. In later airplanes, these 'pusher' propellers were replaced by 'puller' propellers at the front of the plane, which were more efficient.

Engine
The Wrights could not find an engine light and powerful enough for the *Flyer*, so they built their own! The four-cylinder engine weighed 81 kilograms (37 pounds) and produced about 12 horsepower (an average family car engine gives about 80 horsepower).

Pilot's cradle
The pilot lay across the lower wing in a cradle positioned alongside the engine to balance its weight. Cables from the cradle controlled the rudder and wing-warping. The pilot steered by moving his body from side to side, so that the cradle pulled on the control cables.

Elevators
By adjusting the pitch of these mini-wings at the front of the airplane, the pilot could make the *Flyer* climb or descend. On modern airplanes, the elevators are usually at the rear.

Landing runners
The *Flyer* had no undercarriage, but landed on runners, which skidded across the sand.

FIRST FLYERS
On 17 December 1903, Orville and Wilbur Wright, two bicycle engineers from Dayton, Ohio, USA, launched the *Flyer* from sand dunes above the windswept beach at Kitty Hawk, North Carolina. Mounted on a small trolley and with Orville at the controls, the *Flyer's* engine kicked into life, spinning the propellers. Orville released the brake and the *Flyer* raced along the 18-metre (50-foot) take-off track, straight into the wind. There were cheers as the *Flyer* lurched up into the air. It rose to a height of about 3 metres (9 feet) and travelled for 36 metres (100 feet) before plunging down on to the sands. It was little more than a 'hop', but it marked the beginning of the age of the airplane.

WING-WARPING

For the Wright brothers getting an airplane into the sky was only half the challenge. The question remained, how do you steer it once it's airborne? The Wright brothers used a vertical rudder to make the body of the *Flyer* swing to the left or right, but to tilt the wings so that the aircraft could bank, or 'roll', in a smooth turn was more difficult. Wilbur designed a system of control wires that twisted the rear edge of the wingtips slightly when pulled. This 'wing-warping' changed the flow of air over the wings and tilted them, so that the *Flyer* could bank. Today, hinged ailerons do the same job.

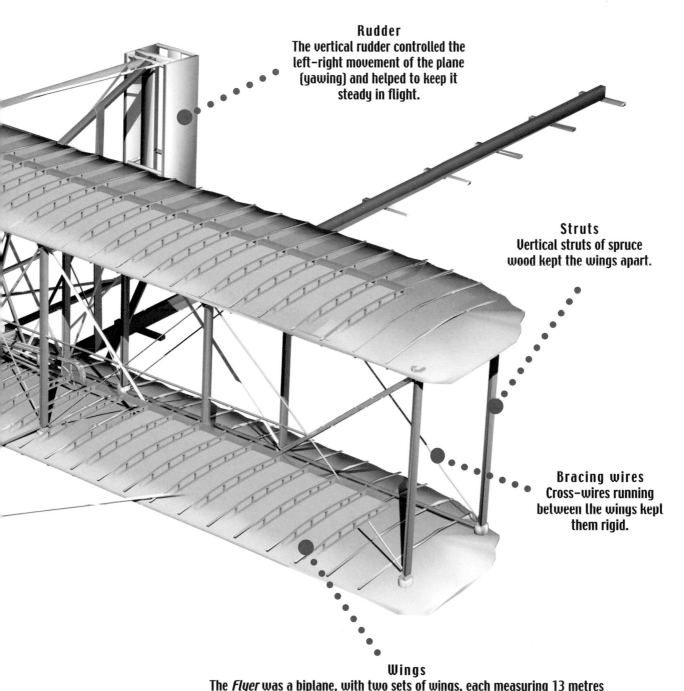

Rudder
The vertical rudder controlled the left-right movement of the plane (yawing) and helped to keep it steady in flight.

Struts
Vertical struts of spruce wood kept the wings apart.

Bracing wires
Cross-wires running between the wings kept them rigid.

Wings
The *Flyer* was a biplane, with two sets of wings, each measuring 13 metres (36 feet) long and 2 metres (6 feet) wide, covered with muslin fabric. Their wooden frame consisted of poles of spruce strengthened by cross-ribs of ash. The ribs were curved, to give the wings an aerofoil shape.

BREITLING ORBITER 3

Burners
The six burners, separated from the capsule by a protective heat shield, generated hot air.

Gas valves
If the pilots wanted to level off or descend, they expelled helium through valves in the top of the gas tanks.

Stores of food, water, and emergency equipment

Cockpit
Using switches on the cockpit's instrument panel, the pilots could operate the burners, change fuel tanks and jettison empty tanks from inside the capsule. For communicating with their base in Geneva, Switzerland, and air-traffic control centres around the world the cockpit was equipped with satellite telephone, radios and a laptop computer to send faxes.

Capsule details
The cramped capsule was made of kevlar (a super-tough plastic) and carbon-fibre. It was well insulated to protect the pilots from the freezing outside temperatures, which sometimes plummeted to –58 ° C. The capsule included sleeping quarters, food and water stores, a toilet and mini-kitchen, oxygen for breathing, and an air-filtering system.

LIGHTER-THAN-AIR CRAFT

The first ever sustained flight was made in 1783 by the French Montgolfier brothers' hot-air balloon. The balloon's envelope was made of paper and hot air was produced by burning straw.

Balloons are basically bags or 'envelopes' of hot air or gas such as hydrogen or helium. In a hot-air balloon, burners heat the air inside the envelope. The air expands as it is heated, which makes it lighter than the air outside and gives the balloon lift. A gas balloon contains gas that is naturally lighter (less dense) than air, so it floats in the atmosphere. Hot-air balloons burn propane or kerosene for fuel. Today, scientists use balloons to carry instruments that gather information about the weather. Other balloons, used for racing and leisure trips, have a basket attached beneath the envelope to carry passengers.

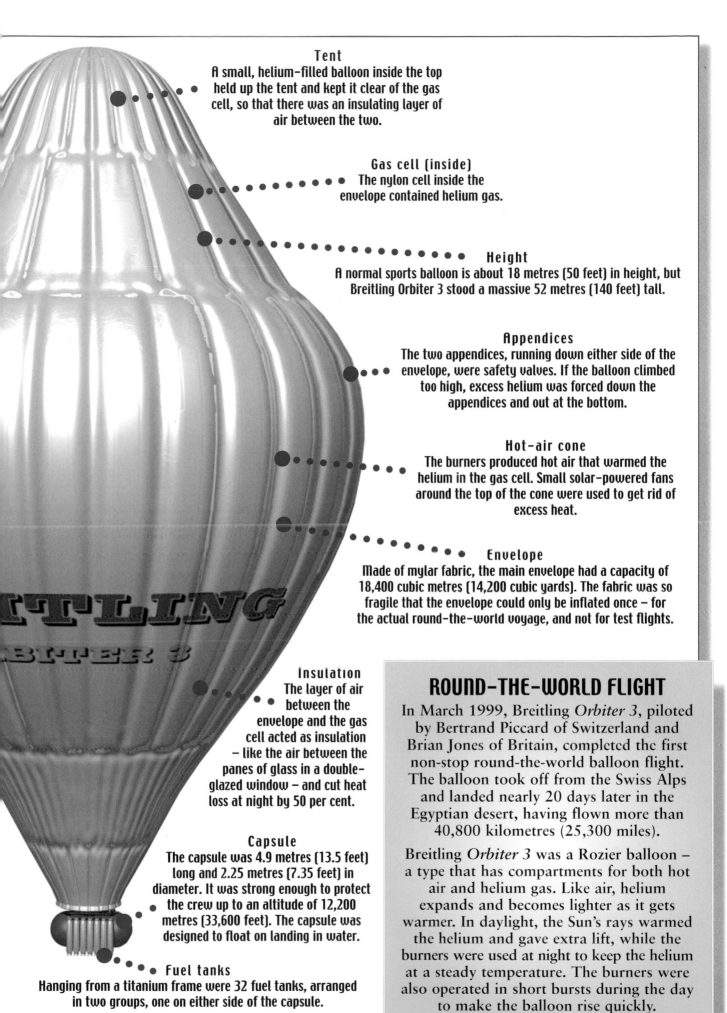

Tent
A small, helium-filled balloon inside the top held up the tent and kept it clear of the gas cell, so that there was an insulating layer of air between the two.

Gas cell (inside)
The nylon cell inside the envelope contained helium gas.

Height
A normal sports balloon is about 18 metres (50 feet) in height, but Breitling Orbiter 3 stood a massive 52 metres (140 feet) tall.

Appendices
The two appendices, running down either side of the envelope, were safety valves. If the balloon climbed too high, excess helium was forced down the appendices and out at the bottom.

Hot-air cone
The burners produced hot air that warmed the helium in the gas cell. Small solar-powered fans around the top of the cone were used to get rid of excess heat.

Envelope
Made of mylar fabric, the main envelope had a capacity of 18,400 cubic metres (14,200 cubic yards). The fabric was so fragile that the envelope could only be inflated once – for the actual round-the-world voyage, and not for test flights.

Insulation
The layer of air between the envelope and the gas cell acted as insulation – like the air between the panes of glass in a double-glazed window – and cut heat loss at night by 50 per cent.

Capsule
The capsule was 4.9 metres (13.5 feet) long and 2.25 metres (7.35 feet) in diameter. It was strong enough to protect the crew up to an altitude of 12,200 metres (33,600 feet). The capsule was designed to float on landing in water.

Fuel tanks
Hanging from a titanium frame were 32 fuel tanks, arranged in two groups, one on either side of the capsule.

ROUND-THE-WORLD FLIGHT

In March 1999, Breitling *Orbiter 3*, piloted by Bertrand Piccard of Switzerland and Brian Jones of Britain, completed the first non-stop round-the-world balloon flight. The balloon took off from the Swiss Alps and landed nearly 20 days later in the Egyptian desert, having flown more than 40,800 kilometres (25,300 miles).

Breitling *Orbiter 3* was a Rozier balloon – a type that has compartments for both hot air and helium gas. Like air, helium expands and becomes lighter as it gets warmer. In daylight, the Sun's rays warmed the helium and gave extra lift, while the burners were used at night to keep the helium at a steady temperature. The burners were also operated in short bursts during the day to make the balloon rise quickly.

HINDENBURG AIRSHIP

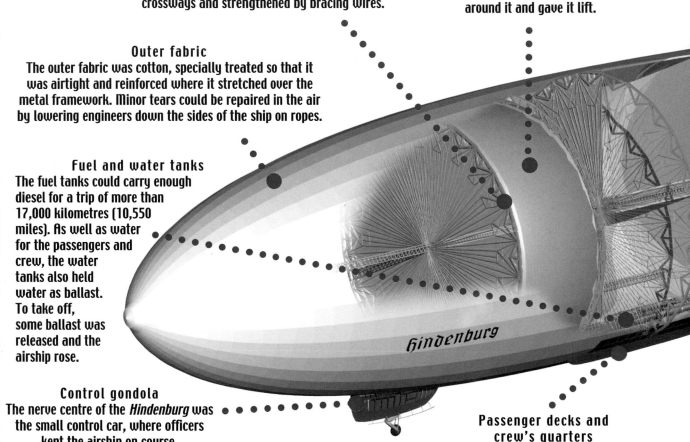

Gas bags
The *Hindenburg* contained 16 air-tight gas bags, made from 1.5 million ox bladders. Wire mesh separated them from the outer fabric and metal framework. The gas bags contained nearly 200,000 cubic metres of highly inflammable hydrogen gas, which made the airship lighter than the air around it and gave it lift.

Framework
The spindly framework, made of a strong aluminium alloy called duralumin, consisted of a series of vertical hoops linked by ribs running crossways and strengthened by bracing wires.

Outer fabric
The outer fabric was cotton, specially treated so that it was airtight and reinforced where it stretched over the metal framework. Minor tears could be repaired in the air by lowering engineers down the sides of the ship on ropes.

Fuel and water tanks
The fuel tanks could carry enough diesel for a trip of more than 17,000 kilometres (10,550 miles). As well as water for the passengers and crew, the water tanks also held water as ballast. To take off, some ballast was released and the airship rose.

Control gondola
The nerve centre of the *Hindenburg* was the small control car, where officers kept the airship on course.

Hindenburg

Passenger decks and crew's quarters

THE AIRSHIP AGE

Airships are lighter-than-air craft which have engines and steering mechanisms. Early airships, built in the late nineteenth century, were cloth-covered, cigar-shaped gas bags, which kept their shape because the gas inside was under high pressure. If the bag sprung a leak, the shape was lost and the airship became difficult to control. So a new type of airship, the 'rigid' was developed, with a strong internal framework made of lightweight metal alloys.

Rigid airships were used in World War I for reconnaissance missions and bombing raids. After the war, they were used to carry passengers on long-distance journeys. In the mid-1930s, airships established the first regular transatlantic air services. Airship travel was expensive and only a small number of passengers could be carried at a time. But airships crossed the Atlantic twice as quickly as the great ocean liners, and the passengers enjoyed an equal level of comfort.

MONSTER OF THE SKIES

Measuring 245 metres (670 feet) long – three times the length of a modern jumbo jet – the German airship *Hindenburg* was the largest craft ever to take to the skies.
On a 50–65-hour transatlantic trip it could carry up to 50 passengers in spacious and luxurious accommodation. The crew usually numbered between 50–60, including 10–15 stewards to look after the passengers' needs.
The *Hindenburg* flew for the first time in 1936, and made 18 successful transatlantic trips in all. It took off on its last voyage from Frankfurt, Germany, on 3 May 1937. Disaster struck when it arrived at Lakehurst, New Jersey, USA, on 6 May. Suddenly, the *Hindenburg* caught fire and exploded in a ball of flame, killing 35 of the 97 people on board. The tragedy signalled the end of the airship age, and these vast giants of the skies were soon replaced on transatlantic voyages by flying-boat airplanes.

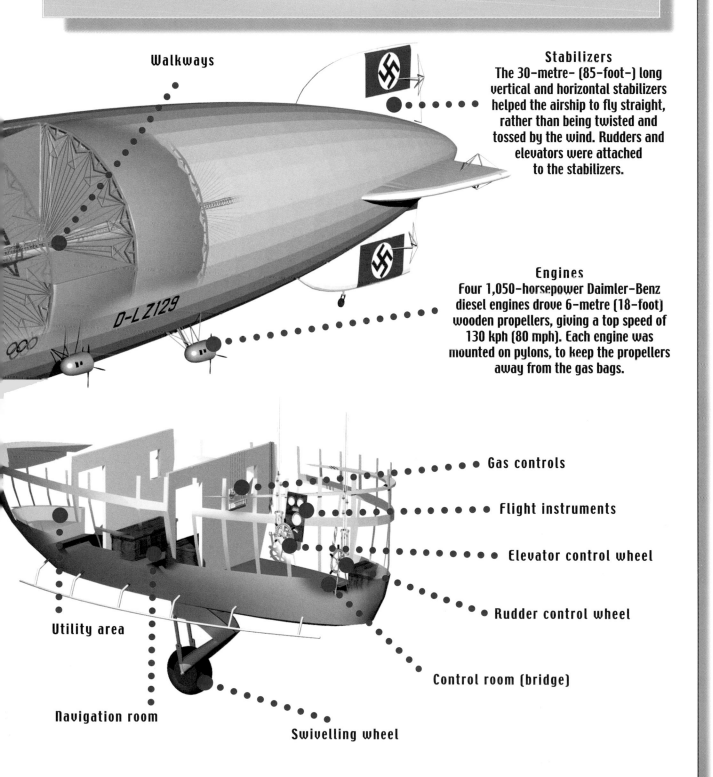

Walkways

Stabilizers
The 30-metre- (85-foot-) long vertical and horizontal stabilizers helped the airship to fly straight, rather than being twisted and tossed by the wind. Rudders and elevators were attached to the stabilizers.

Engines
Four 1,050-horsepower Daimler-Benz diesel engines drove 6-metre (18-foot) wooden propellers, giving a top speed of 130 kph (80 mph). Each engine was mounted on pylons, to keep the propellers away from the gas bags.

D-LZ129

Gas controls

Flight instruments

Elevator control wheel

Rudder control wheel

Control room (bridge)

Utility area

Navigation room

Swivelling wheel

GEE BEE R-2 SUPER SPORTSTER

Fuselage
The fuselage, made of metal and wood, was only 5.4 metres (15 feet) long.

Balancing act
To balance the engine's weight, the pilot and cockpit had to be at the other end of the plane, tucked at the base of the short tail fin.

Flying engine
The R-2 had a 535-horsepower Pratt and Witney R985 engine stuffed into its nose, giving it a top speed of 413 kph (256 mph). The R-1 had a larger 800-horsepower Pratt and Witney R1340 Wasp engine.

Performance
The Super Sportsters performed superbly in knife-edge turns (with the plane tipped on its side) and even upside down. But landing and looping manoeuvres were a little hair-raising for the pilots.

FLYING FOR FUN

After the end of World War I, many pilots turned their flying skills to entertaining the public at airshows. During the 1920s air races were all the rage, with daredevil pilots risking all for big-money prizes. A new breed of airplane emerged, designed purely for speed. Ever larger engines were crammed into smaller and smaller fuselages.

Among the most famous race planes were America's Gee Bee Super Sportsters, built by Granville Brothers of Springfield, Massachusetts. The four brothers began making two-seat biplanes for private use, but then switched to racers. The most famous of these were the R-1 and R-2 Super Sportsters.

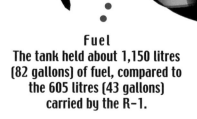

Fuel
The tank held about 1,150 litres (82 gallons) of fuel, compared to the 605 litres (43 gallons) carried by the R-1.

POWERFUL BUT DANGEROUS

The R-1 was little more than an enormous engine bolted on to a tiny body. In 1932, Major James Doolittle piloted the R-1 to victory in the Thompson Trophy race, flying laps around a circuit marked out by pylons. The R-1's sister plane, the R-2, looked almost identical. It had a slightly less powerful but more fuel-efficient engine than the R-1 and a larger fuel tank, allowing it to fly long-distance races with fewer refuelling stops. This gave it a better average speed.

All the Granville Brothers' racers were successful, but only the most skilled flyers could handle them. Over the space of four years, seven Gee Bee racers crashed, killing five pilots, leading to the company ceasing production.

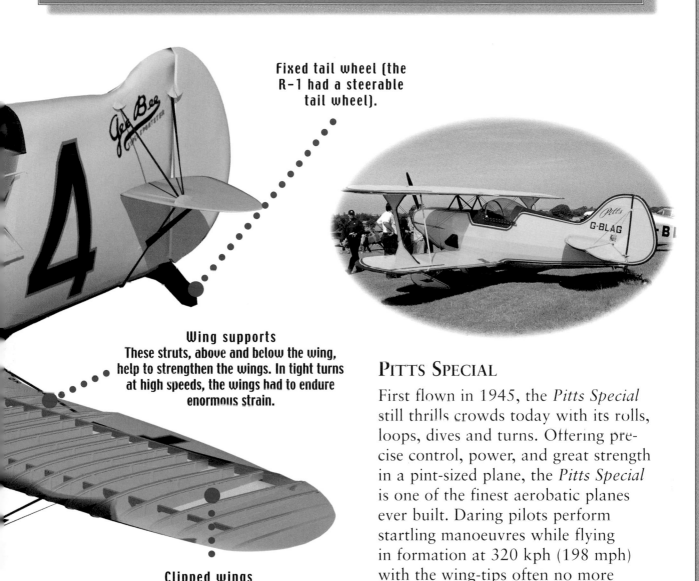

Fixed tail wheel (the R-1 had a steerable tail wheel).

Wing supports
These struts, above and below the wing, help to strengthen the wings. In tight turns at high speeds, the wings had to endure enormous strain.

Clipped wings
The R-2's wing-span was just 7.6 metres (21 feet).

PITTS SPECIAL

First flown in 1945, the *Pitts Special* still thrills crowds today with its rolls, loops, dives and turns. Offering precise control, power, and great strength in a pint-sized plane, the *Pitts Special* is one of the finest aerobatic planes ever built. Daring pilots perform startling manoeuvres while flying in formation at 320 kph (198 mph) with the wing-tips often no more than 3 metres (8 feet) apart!

FATAL FLIGHTS

The planes were said to be dangerous – and they were. Both the R-1 and R-2 crashed in 1933. The parts were salvaged and reused in the form of the R-1/R-2, which had a larger fuel tank set further back than before. This upset the plane's balance, making it impossible to control – it crashed on its first flight killing its pilot, Allen Granville.

BOEING 314 CLIPPER

Navigation dome
To check the plane was on course on long ocean flights, where there were no familiar landmarks or coastlines, navigators would look out of this dome and note the positions of stars.

Upper deck
This contained the flight deck, the crew's quarters, and compartments for cargo and the passengers' luggage.

Baggage compartment

Engines
Four massive 1,600-horsepower Wright GR-2600 Double-Cyclone radial engines gave a top speed of 340 kph (210 mph) and a cruising speed of 302 kph (190 mph). The Clipper could fly more than 5,900 kilometres (3,700 miles) without refuelling.

Radio operator's seat

Flight deck
The Clipper's flight deck was the largest ever built.

Galley (kitchen)
The in-flight food was of the highest order. Chefs recruited from top hotels oversaw preparation at the flying boat terminal and the meals were cooked in the galley during the flight. At mealtimes, the tables were set with fine china and silver cutlery. Two waiters served the hungry diners.

Fuselage
The all-metal fuselage, nearly 6 metres (9 feet) deep and shaped like the hull of a ship, was designed to float and move easily through the water.

Sponsons
These floats projected from the sides of the plane and balanced the aircraft on the water. They helped to give extra lift in the air, and were also used to hold fuel. Most other flying boats and seaplanes had floats under the wings.

PLANES THAT FLOAT

The huge flying boats of the late 1930s sped across the water on their take-off run. They established the first long-distance airline routes across the world's oceans. These journeys were beyond the range of conventional airplanes, which could not carry enough fuel. But flying boats were able to cross oceans by refuelling at harbours and islands as they went. The largest commercial flying boat was the Boeing 314, which entered service in March 1939.

During World War II (1939–1945), flying boats were used to hunt enemy submarines and rescue pilots. After the war, the flying boats found themselves competing with fast, reliable airliners on long-distance passenger routes. As the flying boats were much more expensive to run, they were gradually phased out.

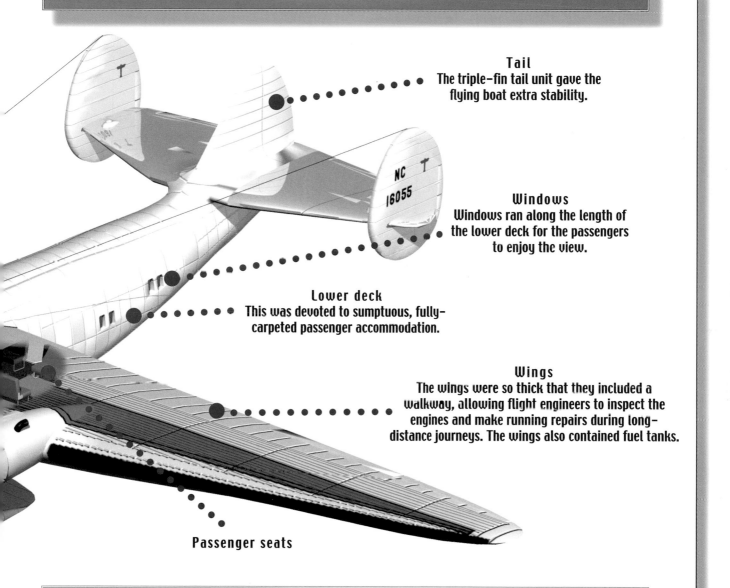

Tail
The triple-fin tail unit gave the flying boat extra stability.

Windows
Windows ran along the length of the lower deck for the passengers to enjoy the view.

Lower deck
This was devoted to sumptuous, fully-carpeted passenger accommodation.

Wings
The wings were so thick that they included a walkway, allowing flight engineers to inspect the engines and make running repairs during long-distance journeys. The wings also contained fuel tanks.

Passenger seats

THE MIGHTY CLIPPER

America's Boeing 314 was designed to carry around 75 day passengers, or 35–40 in sleeping berths on long-distance flights. The 10-man crew included two pilots, a navigator, a flight engineer, a radio operator, the ship's master (an officer who commanded the plane but did not fly it) and a relief crew of four.

Pan American Airways operated a fleet of Boeing 314s – called 'Clippers' after the fast sailing vessels of the nineteenth century – on routes across the Atlantic and Pacific. A Clipper's transatlantic journey from New York to Europe took about 24 hours, including two stops en-route. The flight across the Pacific, from San Francisco to Hong Kong, took five or six days, with rest and refuelling stops on Hawaii and other Pacific islands.

BOEING B-17 FLYING FORTRESS

Engine power
The B-17 had four turbocharged, air-cooled Wright R-1820-97 Cyclone engines. They were radial engines, which means that their nine cylinders were arranged in a circle around the crankshaft. Each gave 1,200 horsepower, allowing the B-17 to reach a maximum speed of just over 460 kph (285 mph). The cruising speed with a full bomb load was around 240 kph (150 mph).

Astro-navigation dome
For night-flying missions, the navigator would look out of this dome to check star positions.

Dorsal gun-turret
Mounted on top of the flight deck, this turret gave protection against fighters diving out of the Sun.

Bombardier
Sitting in the nose of the plane, the bombardier used a bomb-sight to look through the flat viewing panel in the plastic cone and make sure that the bombs were released at just the right moment. Under fire from anti-aircraft guns or enemy fighters, the bombardier needed a steady nerve to hit the target.

Nose cone
This was made of single-piece moulded plastic and fitted with machine guns, one on either side.

Chin turret
The twin guns were remote-controlled from inside the nose-cone.

Bombs
The B-17 normally carried 2.7 tonnes (2.7 tons) of bombs, but it could manage up to 6.2 tonnes (6.1 tons) if necessary. The bombs were held in vertical racks in the bomb bay.

Undercarriage
The B-17's retractable undercarriage consisted of two large main wheels, one under each wing, and a smaller one near the tail.

BRISTLING WITH GUNS

World War II saw fighters and bombers develop by leaps and bounds to become fearsome military weapons. Huge formations of bombers caused massive destruction, and one of the most successful was the American Boeing B-17. Bombers were much slower than fighters and so were sitting targets for fast, agile enemy planes armed with machine guns and cannons. To counteract this threat, machine guns were mounted in almost every conceivable position on the B-17. In fact, the B-17 so bristled with armaments that one newspaper reporter called it a 'flying fortress' – and the name stuck!

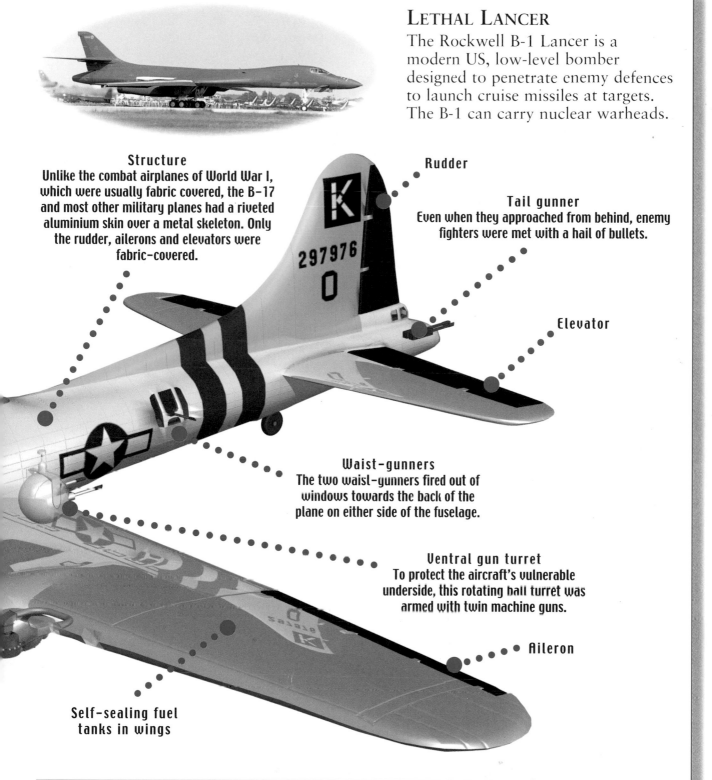

LETHAL LANCER
The Rockwell B-1 Lancer is a modern US, low-level bomber designed to penetrate enemy defences to launch cruise missiles at targets. The B-1 can carry nuclear warheads.

Structure
Unlike the combat airplanes of World War I, which were usually fabric covered, the B-17 and most other military planes had a riveted aluminium skin over a metal skeleton. Only the rudder, ailerons and elevators were fabric-covered.

Rudder

Tail gunner
Even when they approached from behind, enemy fighters were met with a hail of bullets.

Elevator

Waist-gunners
The two waist-gunners fired out of windows towards the back of the plane on either side of the fuselage.

Ventral gun turret
To protect the aircraft's vulnerable underside, this rotating ball turret was armed with twin machine guns.

Aileron

Self-sealing fuel tanks in wings

297976
O

DAYLIGHT DANGER
Thousands of B-17s took part in daylight bombing raids over Europe, dropping more than 580,600 tonnes (571,450 tons) of high explosives on enemy targets. But daylight bombing made them vulnerable and initially many fell victim to German fighters. The B-17s' best defence was for large numbers of planes to fly in tight formation, so that fighters attacking from any direction faced a volley of fire from several aircraft. Flying like this, they managed to shoot down countless enemy planes.

The introduction of long-range escort fighters, such as the American P-51 Mustang, turned the tables. This allowed the B-17s to concentrate on their bombing missions while the escorts – their 'little friends', as the B-17 crews called them – dealt with enemy fighters.

BOEING 747-400 'JUMBO JET'

Class act
As in most airliners, there are different classes of seats, all priced differently and offering different levels of comfort and service. The cheapest seats are economy class, with business class being more spacious, and first class offering the best facilities – and costing the most!

Fuel tanks
Situated in the wings and the tail-planes, the tanks hold over 216,840 litres (15,400 gallons) of fuel.

Flight deck
Dials and gauges have been replaced by six computer screens displaying all the key data the flight crew need to fly the plane. For most of the journey the computer 'autopilot' flies the plane, with the flight crew assuming control for take-off and landing. A relief crew of two may accompany the pilot and co-pilot on long-haul trips.

Washrooms
Passengers can freshen up on long, exhausting journeys.

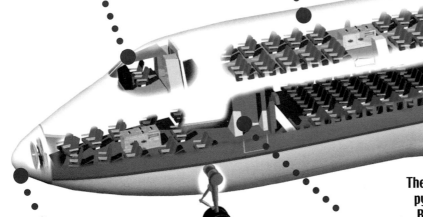

Engine pods
The four pods suspended from wing pylons each carry a Rolls-Royce RB-211-524H turbofan engine.

Nose cone
This houses the weather radar scanner.

Galley
Meals are prepared on the ground before take-off and heated up in the galley during the flight.

THE JET AGE

In 1952, Britain's De Havilland Comet, the world's first jet airliner, entered service. The jet engine has no pistons but burns a fuel-air mixture in a combustion chamber. A jet of hot exhaust gases rushes out from the rear of the engine, providing thrust to push the plane forward. The air is squeezed by a compressor as it enters the engine. The compressor is driven by a set of turbine blades, which is why it is normally called a turbojet engine. Most modern jet engines have a huge fan in front to suck more air into the engine and give extra power. These are known as turbofan engines. They are quieter and burn less fuel than turbojets.

ELEPHANTINE AIRPLANE

As more people could afford to travel by air, ever more aircraft were needed to cope with the rising levels of passengers. To prevent the airports and skies from being gridlocked with air traffic, wide-bodied, high-capacity jets were developed. Foremost among the wide-bodied jets is the Boeing 747, nicknamed the 'Jumbo' because of its huge size. When it entered service in 1970, it was twice as heavy and powerful as any other airliner, and could carry double the number of passengers. The 747-400, the most recent model, carries just over 420 passengers on long-haul international flights, not forgetting all their luggage, plus fuel for the plane and food for the journey, and the crew.

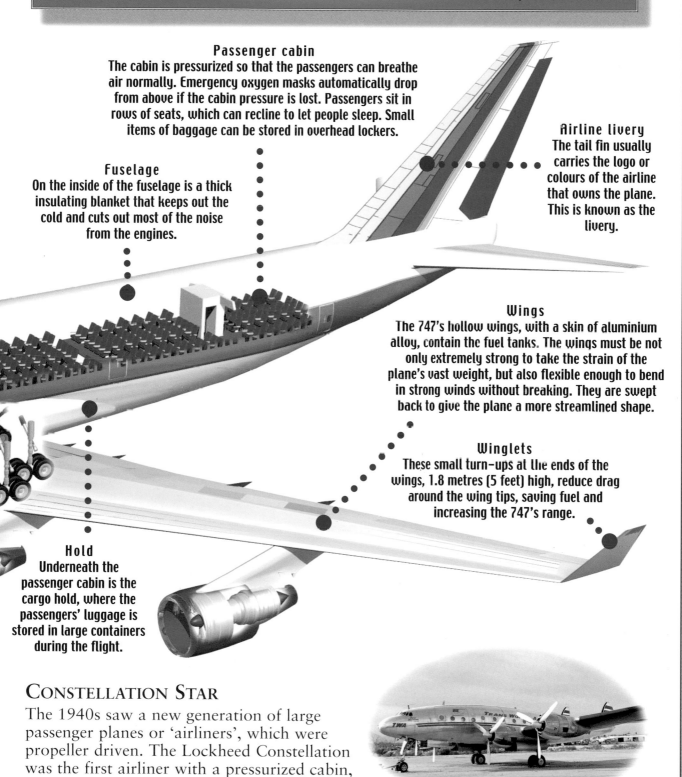

Passenger cabin
The cabin is pressurized so that the passengers can breathe air normally. Emergency oxygen masks automatically drop from above if the cabin pressure is lost. Passengers sit in rows of seats, which can recline to let people sleep. Small items of baggage can be stored in overhead lockers.

Airline livery
The tail fin usually carries the logo or colours of the airline that owns the plane. This is known as the livery.

Fuselage
On the inside of the fuselage is a thick insulating blanket that keeps out the cold and cuts out most of the noise from the engines.

Wings
The 747's hollow wings, with a skin of aluminium alloy, contain the fuel tanks. The wings must be not only extremely strong to take the strain of the plane's vast weight, but also flexible enough to bend in strong winds without breaking. They are swept back to give the plane a more streamlined shape.

Winglets
These small turn-ups at the ends of the wings, 1.8 metres (5 feet) high, reduce drag around the wing tips, saving fuel and increasing the 747's range.

Hold
Underneath the passenger cabin is the cargo hold, where the passengers' luggage is stored in large containers during the flight.

CONSTELLATION STAR

The 1940s saw a new generation of large passenger planes or 'airliners', which were propeller driven. The Lockheed Constellation was the first airliner with a pressurized cabin, enabling it to fly above bad weather and give passengers a more comfortable ride.

McDONNELL DOUGLAS AH-64 APACHE

Crew
The co-pilot/gunner sits in front of and below the pilot, in an armoured cockpit.

Power plant
Behind the rotor, and to either side of the fuselage, are the two 1,696 horsepower General Electric T700-GE-701C turbines. They give the Apache a top speed of around 300 kph (186 mph).

Main rotor
The four-blade rotor, with a diameter of 14.6 metres (40 feet), creates the helicopter's lift. The stainless steel and fibreglass blades have swept edges.

Controls
There are three main controls. The control column is operated to tilt the main rotor to go forwards, backwards or sideways. The collective pitch lever is operated to change the pitch of the rotor blades, making the helicopter go up, down, or hover. Control pedals in the floor adjust the pitch of the tail-blades to turn left or right.

Nose assembly
The all-weather, day and night weapon-sighting equipment is mounted in the nose, and includes a TV camera, laser tracker, and forward-looking infrared sensor.

Chin gun
Aimed by the co-pilot/gunner, the 30-millimetre M230 Chin Gun has 1,200 rounds of ammunition.

Weaponry
The stubby wings provide four 'hard points' to which weapons can be attached. The Apache's favoured armoury is Rockwell AGM-114 Hellfire anti-tank missiles and rocket launchers loaded with 70-millimetre FFAR rockets. Usually it carries a combination of both. Extra fuel tanks or alternative armaments could also be attached to the hard points.

AWESOME APACHE

The Apache is a two-seat, anti-tank attack helicopter whose armoury can include guns, missiles and rockets. The helicopter can be a devastating weapon on the battlefield, hovering out of sight behind trees or buildings and then popping up unexpectedly to send a hail of rockets on to an enemy tank. Sometimes helicopters work in pairs, with one helicopter highlighting the target with a laser beam and guiding the other's missiles on to their target. Equipped with sensitive electronic devices, it can fight in daytime, at night, and in poor weather.

ROTARY WINGS

Helicopters are the most versatile of all aircraft, able to hover, take off and land vertically, and fly backwards and sideways, as well as forwards. Their rotor blades are like spinning wings. The blades are aerofoil-shaped and slightly angled. The angle of the blades is known as the pitch. The whirring blades push the air downwards and generate lift. The steeper the pitch of the blades, the greater the lift they give. When the lift is greater than the helicopter's weight, the aircraft takes off. When lift and weight are equal, the helicopter hovers, and when weight is greater than lift, the helicopter descends.

Using the controls, the pilot tilts the entire set of rotor blades forwards, giving thrust that pushes the helicopter along. To move sideways or backwards, the pilot simply tilts the blades in the desired direction. Changing the pitch of the tail-rotor blades turns the helicopter left or right.

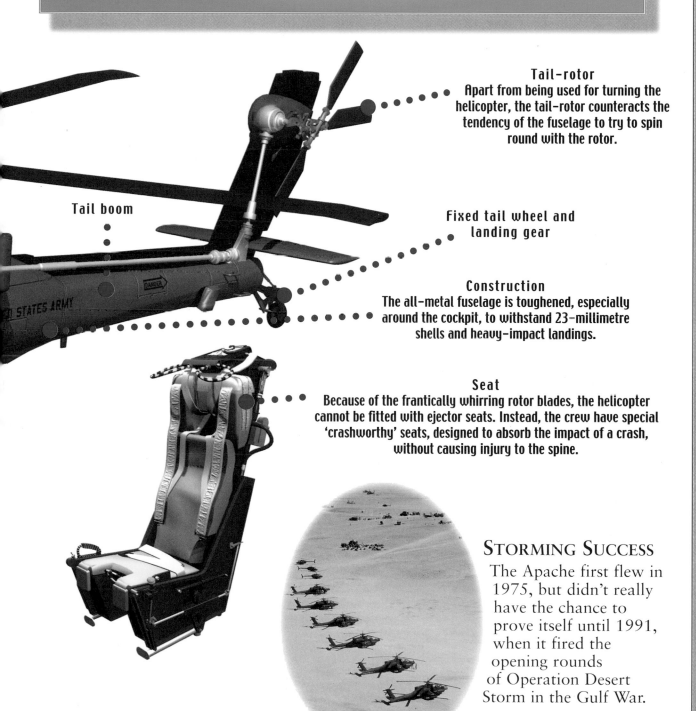

Tail boom

Tail-rotor
Apart from being used for turning the helicopter, the tail-rotor counteracts the tendency of the fuselage to try to spin round with the rotor.

Fixed tail wheel and landing gear

Construction
The all-metal fuselage is toughened, especially around the cockpit, to withstand 23-millimetre shells and heavy-impact landings.

Seat
Because of the frantically whirring rotor blades, the helicopter cannot be fitted with ejector seats. Instead, the crew have special 'crashworthy' seats, designed to absorb the impact of a crash, without causing injury to the spine.

STORMING SUCCESS
The Apache first flew in 1975, but didn't really have the chance to prove itself until 1991, when it fired the opening rounds of Operation Desert Storm in the Gulf War.

BOEING VERTOL CHINOOK CH-47

Capacity
The Chinook is extremely spacious inside, with a cabin measuring 2.3 metres (6 feet) wide, 2 metres (5 feet) high and over 9 metres (25 feet) long. It can carry 44 fully equipped troops or 24 injured soldiers on stretchers, along with medical attendants.

Turning technique
The fibreglass blades can spin at up to 225 times per minute. Because the Chinook doesn't have a tail-rotor, it needs another mechanism to turn the craft. Normally the speeds of the two rotors are the same so they balance each other out. But making one rotor spin faster or slower than the other turns the helicopter to the left or the right.

Cockpit
Two pilots and two crew sit in the cockpit. The cockpit seats have vibration absorbers to smooth the ride and reduce pilot fatigue. The flying controls are hydraulically powered.

Strong blast
The downrush of air from the Chinook's powerful rotors is equivalent to wind speeds of 90 kph (56 mph) – enough to blow a Cessna 172 on to its back!

Weapons
The Chinook rarely carries weapons, but it can if necessary. Armaments can include machine guns, and grenade and rocket launchers.

WORKHORSE OF THE SKY

When you need to get large numbers of troops, emergency supplies or heavy machinery into awkward places – call for the Chinook! The 15-tonne (about 15-ton) Boeing Vertol CH-47 Chinook is probably the most reliable and popular heavy-lifting helicopter in the world. First introduced in 1961, it has been constantly updated and is still in service with most modern armed forces.

Under its belly, the Chinook has three crane hooks for lifting heavy objects. The front and back hooks can lift up to 5 tonnes (5 tons), but the central crane hook can raise loads in excess of 9 tonnes (9 tons), though not over great distances. The cargo is usually armoured vehicles, field guns and battlefield supplies. Three loads can be moved at once by using cables of different lengths so that the loads do not collide in flight.

Drive shaft
This carries power from engines to front rotor.

Deadly blades
The Chinook's rotor span is 18.3 metres (50 feet). Approach from the front and you risk decapitation, as the blades. can skim to 1.2 metres (3 feet) off the ground! At the rear, clearance is 5.4 metres (15 feet).

Engines
The twin Lycoming T55-L712 turbines give a top speed of 306 kph (190 mph). A compressor first squeezes the intake air. The air is then mixed with fuel, and the mixture burned in a combustion chamber. The waste gases drive a set of turbine blades which, in turn, power the rotors.

Cargo ramp
The ramp descends at the rear of the helicopter for fast loading and unloading.

Undercarriage
Two pairs of landing wheels give stability when the Chinook is fully laden.

Floating Wokka
The fuselage is watertight in case the Chinook comes down in the ocean.

Fuel supply
The large tanks under the cabin floor hold enough fuel for up to 10 hours flying, depending on the load.

BLACK HAWK
The Sikorsky Black Hawk is a multi-role transport helicopter, used to carry troops and equipment to the battlefield.

MIGHTY WOKKA!
The Chinook does not have a tail-rotor, but it counteracts the fuselage's tendency to spin round by having two very large main rotors, each turning in a different direction. The sound they make – a deafening 'wokka wokka' – is the origin of the Chinook's nickname: the Mighty Wokka.

The rotors are over 15 metres (41 feet) in diameter and actually overlap in the middle. The rear one is higher than the front one, and the two are linked by a gearing arrangement that ensures that they do not strike each other – which would be disastrous. The rotors are powered by two powerful engines at the rear of the helicopter. The Chinook has also been used as a passenger helicopter to make short trips between cities, and to carry personnel to and from oil rigs far out at sea.

BRITISH AEROSPACE /BOEING HARRIER

JUMP JET

In a tight dog-fight with enemy fighters, manoeuvrability is more valuable than speed. The Harrier is a V/STOL (Vertical/Short Take-Off and Landing) fighter and strike airplane. It can take off and fly straight upwards, and land by coming straight back down. If it has a heavy load, the Harrier takes a short run-up to help it 'jump' into the air.

Wings
The short, backward-sloping wings have a span of just 9.25 metres (25 feet). They are 'shoulder wings', which means that they are joined to the plane at the top of the fuselage.

Engine air-intake
There are two semicircular air-intakes, one on either side of the fuselage. A large fan at the front sucks air into the engine.

Engine
The Harrier is powered by a single Rolls-Royce Pegasus vectored-thrust turbofan engine located in the centre of the plane. Hatches just behind the cockpit give easy access for repairs and maintenance.

Nose cone
This contains sensors that can lock laser- and TV-guided weapons on to their targets.

Cockpit
The cockpit is equipped with a head-up display, video-screen information displays, a digital moving map, and night-vision goggles for the pilot.

Ejector seat
The pilot sits in a rocket-powered ejector seat unit, which has an oxygen mask, a parachute for descent to the ground and a rubber dinghy in case of a watery landing.

Cannon pods
The Harrier has two 30-millimetre cannon pods, one on each side of the plane's belly.

Main landing wheels
These descend from the centre of the fuselage.

Front engine nozzles
These expel cold air drawn in by the front fan.

Rear engine nozz
These expel hot gases burning fuel in the en

22

Materials
The Harrier's fuselage and wings are built from light, strong aluminium alloys and 'composite' materials such as carbon-fibre.

Avionics
Much of the 'hardware' for the electronic flight equipment, called avionics, is housed in the rear part of the fuselage.

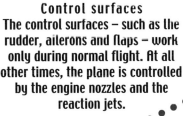

NOT FAST BUT DEADLY
The Harrier is not a fast airplane, with a top speed of about 1,200 kph (745 mph), but it is very agile. It can fly backwards, or from side to side, and it can even hover. It can also slow down from 1,000 kph (620 mph) to a virtual standstill in about 12 seconds.

Reaction jets
The main engine is too powerful for fine manoeuvres at low speeds, so the plane has small compressed-air 'puffers', called reaction jets. Located in the nose, wing-tips, and tail, the reaction jets are fed pressurized air from the compressor in the main engine.

Control surfaces
The control surfaces – such as the rudder, ailerons and flaps – work only during normal flight. At all other times, the plane is controlled by the engine nozzles and the reaction jets.

Wing wheels
Towards each wing-tip, away from the exhaust jets from the engine nozzles, the Harrier has a small wheel. Mounted on shock-absorbing legs, these wheels steady the plane during take-off and landing. The wheels fold back when the plane is flying.

Hard point/pylon
Missiles, bombs and extra fuel tanks are carried on the hard points (also called pylons). The Harrier can be fitted with up to nine hard points on the wings and fuselage.

VECTORED THRUST
The secret of the Harrier's success is its 'vectored thrust'. This is the ability to control and direct gases leaving the engine. The single jet engine has four rotating (vectoring) exhaust nozzles, just under where the wings meet the fuselage. For a vertical take-off, the nozzles point towards the ground, directing the gases downwards so that the plane is pushed up into the air. As the Harrier gains height, the nozzles swivel to point diagonally downwards, so that the gases push the plane both up and forwards. For normal flight the nozzles are directed backwards, and as the Harrier is propelled forwards the flow of air over the wings provides lift to keep the plane airborne. To fly backwards, the nozzles point down and slightly forwards.

A-10 THUNDERBOLT

Fuel tanks
The fuel is kept in special foam chambers that prevent fumes from forming. This lessens the risk of fire if the fuel tanks are damaged. The tanks are hidden right in the centre of the plane and protected by fire-detectors and extinguishers.

Canopy
The large bubble-shaped canopy gives good all-round vision. Its toughened glass can withstand small-arms fire.

Cockpit
The single pilot sits in a protective 'bathtub' made of ultra-strong titanium-alloy. The cockpit is filled with a host of switches, gauges and dials. During training, every pilot must pass a blindfold test in which they have to find and activate controls by touch alone.

Head-up display (HUD)
Modern combat aircraft often have a see-through screen that displays important flight information in front of the pilot's face. The pilot can read the details without having to look down at the flight instruments. HUDs can also be used for aiming guns or missiles at targets. Some pilot helmets have a special visor that does the same job as the HUD.

Boarding ladder

Ammunition belt and drum
Shells are fed to the cannon by the ammunition belt. The drum in the plane's belly carries 1,174 rounds of ammunition. It also collects the used shell-cases to prevent them flying into the engine's fans.

Rotary cannon
Slung beneath the cockpit is the single Avenger cannon, whose seven rotating barrels shoot bursts of high-velocity 30-millimetre high-explosive or armour-piercing shells. A short burst is all that is needed to put a tank out of action. The noise of the firing cannon gave it its nickname – the 'burp gun'.

ROVING DESTROYER
The A-10's role is to support ground forces. The A-10 entered service in 1976 and proved its worth to devastating effect in the Gulf War of 1990 and during the Kosovo conflict of 1999. The A-10 is slow compared to most combat airplanes, with poor acceleration, but the straight wings give tremendous lift and make it very agile at low speeds and low altitudes. They also allow it to take off and land on short runways built close to the combat zone. It can still fly with an entire engine shot off its mounting, one rudder missing, or a large chunk of a wing blown away in combat!

LINGERING THREAT

The A-10 lingers over the battlefield making low-level jinking runs, often at tree-top height, to attack tanks and other armoured vehicles.

Tail
The twin tail fins are designed to improve low-speed manoeuvrability. They also help to conceal the engine's hot exhaust gases from heat-seeking infrared missiles, making the A-10 a harder target for the missiles to lock on to.

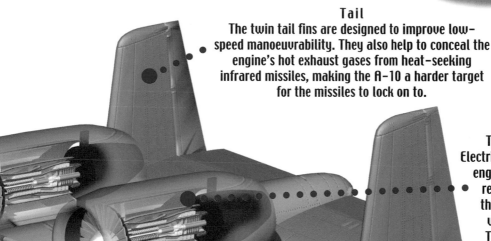

Engines
The A-10 has two General Electric TF34-GE-100 turbofan engines mounted high on the rear of the fuselage so that the pilot has an unhindered view of the terrain below. The engines give the A-10 a top speed when fully loaded of 725 kph (450 mph) and a cruising speed of 555 kph (345 mph).

Ailerons
The special split ailerons help to stabilize the plane in flight as it blasts enemy tanks with its powerful cannon.

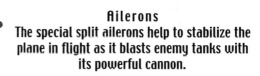

Weapons payload
The 11 pylons, three under the fuselage and four under each wing, can carry over 7,250 kilograms (3,300 pounds) of weapons or equipment. Weaponry can include rockets, air-to-air and air-to-ground guided missiles, and free-fall and guided bombs. The A-10 can also carry electronic countermeasures (ECM) pods, which contain transmitters that jam enemy radar.

Undercarriage
In flight, the wheels only partly retract. In the event of a crash-landing, they may help to lessen the impact, limiting damage to plane and pilot.

FLYING PIG

The pilots who fly the strange-looking A-10 nickname it the 'Warthog', after the fierce, ugly African wild pig. Like its animal namesake, the Warthog is not to be messed with. The A-10 was designed around its gun – a fearsome 6-metre (18-foot) long cannon that can spit out shells at a rate of up to 4,200 per minute. The cannon shoots straight ahead. This means that pilots have to fly directly towards targets, often facing flak (anti-aircraft fire) full on, so the A-10 needs to be tough – and it is! Titanium armour plating, up to 38 millimetres (1.5 inches) thick, surrounds the cockpit, and also helps to protect the engines and some of the flight control systems. The A-10 can survive direct hits from armour-piercing shells and high-explosive projectiles.

GRUMMAN HAWKEYE

Rotodome
Measuring about 8 metres (22 feet) in diameter, the motor-driven radar disc, or 'rotodome', revolves five times per minute. Hydraulic jacks raise the rotodome for AEW patrols and lower it when the plane is out of action.

Fins and rudders
While the fuselage and wings are metal, the fins and rudders are largely fibreglass, to reduce radar reflection.

Chemical toilet
Even the best trained aircrew need to use the bathroom from time to time!

Control centre
The three systems operators – radar operator, air control officer and combat information officer – sit facing electronic display panels along the fuselage wall. The seats swivel to face forwards when taking off and landing.

Catapult tow-bar
Airplanes are launched from carriers by catapults, which hurl the planes from a standing start to speeds of around 320 kph (200 mph). For take-off, the tow-bar is attached to the catapult, which runs along a track in the deck.

SPY IN THE SKY

The Grumman Hawkeye is an airborne early warning (AEW) airplane. It may look as though it's carrying its own parasol, but the huge disc on top of the plane is actually a rotating radar antenna that scours the skies and seas for unfriendly intruders. Bristling with sophisticated electronic equipment, the Hawkeye can track over 2,000 aircraft, missiles, and ships simultaneously. It can detect and identify bomber-sized targets as far as 530 kilometres (330 miles) away – not bad for an airplane that made its maiden flight about 40 years ago! The E-2C II is the latest upgrade of the basic Hawkeye structure, and the Hawkeye 2000, currently under development, will continue to be the airborne eyes and ears of the US Navy for many years to come.

RADAR RECONNAISSANCE

The Hawkeyes travel with a fleet of naval ships on board an aircraft carrier. Once airborne, they can fly beyond the range of the carrier's own radar, giving a vast coverage of sky and sea. In a combat situation, they can give fighter pilots an idea of the 'big picture' of what's going on in an air battle, and alert them to threats and targets coming their way. The plane has a crew of five: two pilots, and three systems operators who analyse the data collected by the plane's monitoring equipment and communicate with the carrier and other aircraft.

Vital statistics
The Hawkeye is nearly 17.6 metres (48 feet) long, 5.6 metres (15 feet) high and has a wing-span of about 24.6 metres (8 feet).

Wings
When not in use, hydraulic jacks fold the wings back so that the Hawkeye does not take up too much space on the crowded carrier deck, and can fit on to the lifts that descend to the hangers below deck.

Engines
Two Allison T56-A-427 turboprop engines, mounted either side of the fuselage on the high, straight wings, drive the four-bladed composite propellers.

Cooling system
This intake duct houses the vapour-cycle radiator, which controls the temperature inside the plane. An efficient cooling system is needed, because the mass of electronic equipment on board the Hawkeye generates a lot of heat.

Hardware
The electronic hardware for all the Hawkeye's systems is packed into the area behind the pilot's cockpit.

Cockpit
The side windows bulge outwards so the pilots can get a good downward view. The windscreen is electrically heated, to prevent ice formation. Parachutes are located behind the pilots' seats.

GUIDE IN THE SKY
Hawkeyes are always the first planes to take off from an aircraft carrier and the last to land. They act as 'flying control towers' for other aircraft launched from the carrier, such as this Northrop Grumman F-14 Tomcat. The Hawkeyes guide their flight to and from the ship.

NORTH AMERICAN X-15

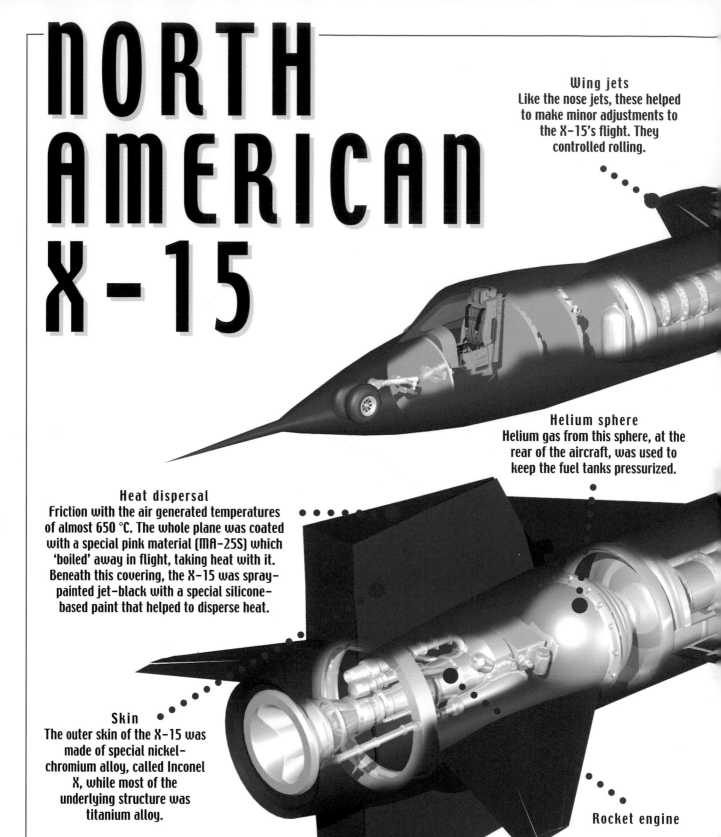

Wing jets
Like the nose jets, these helped to make minor adjustments to the X–15's flight. They controlled rolling.

Helium sphere
Helium gas from this sphere, at the rear of the aircraft, was used to keep the fuel tanks pressurized.

Heat dispersal
Friction with the air generated temperatures of almost 650 °C. The whole plane was coated with a special pink material (MA–25S) which 'boiled' away in flight, taking heat with it. Beneath this covering, the X–15 was spray-painted jet–black with a special silicone-based paint that helped to disperse heat.

Skin
The outer skin of the X–15 was made of special nickel-chromium alloy, called Inconel X, while most of the underlying structure was titanium alloy.

Rocket engine

X-PLANES

Many unusual-looking experimental aircraft, often called X-planes, have been built for research into high speed flight. One of the most famous X-planes was the Bell X-1. Flown by Captain Charles 'Chuck' Yeager, it became the first plane to fly faster than the speed of sound in October 1947, when it reached 1,078 kph (668 mph). Perhaps the most amazing X-plane of all was the dart-shaped North American X-15. This rocket-powered plane was used in the 1960s to investigate flight at hypersonic speeds (at least five times faster than the speed of sound).

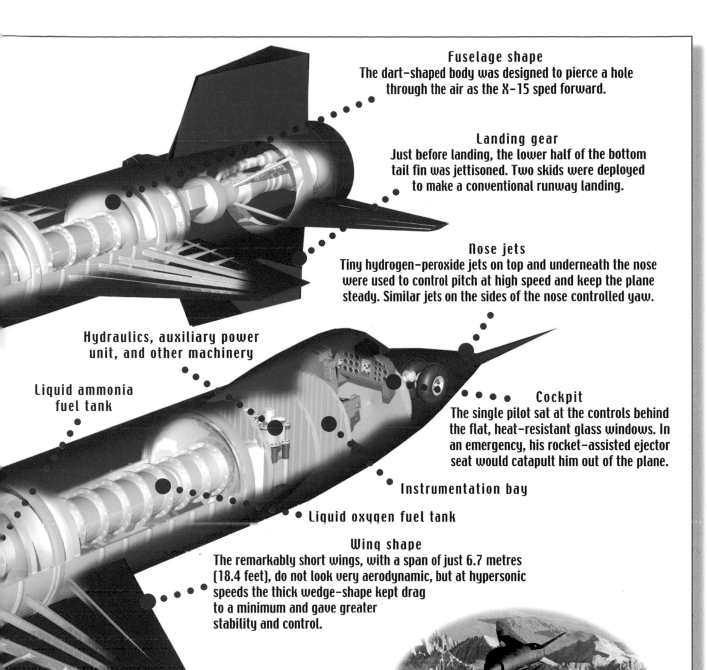

Fuselage shape
The dart-shaped body was designed to pierce a hole through the air as the X-15 sped forward.

Landing gear
Just before landing, the lower half of the bottom tail fin was jettisoned. Two skids were deployed to make a conventional runway landing.

Nose jets
Tiny hydrogen-peroxide jets on top and underneath the nose were used to control pitch at high speed and keep the plane steady. Similar jets on the sides of the nose controlled yaw.

Hydraulics, auxiliary power unit, and other machinery

Liquid ammonia fuel tank

Cockpit
The single pilot sat at the controls behind the flat, heat-resistant glass windows. In an emergency, his rocket-assisted ejector seat would catapult him out of the plane.

Instrumentation bay

Liquid oxygen fuel tank

Wing shape
The remarkably short wings, with a span of just 6.7 metres (18.4 feet), do not look very aerodynamic, but at hypersonic speeds the thick wedge-shape kept drag to a minimum and gave greater stability and control.

INCREDIBLE SPEED

Apart from rocket-powered craft such as the X-15, no conventional airplane has flown faster than the Lockheed SR-71 Blackbird, which reached nearly 3,530 kph (2,190 mph) in 1976. The Blackbird was used for secret reconnaissance missions by the US air force, but has now been withdrawn from service.

THE EDGE OF SPACE

The X-15 was carried into the air by a modified B-52 Stratofortress bomber and released at a high altitude. Once the X-15 was clear of the 'parent' plane, the pilot fired the rocket engine, which burned liquid ammonia fuel with liquid oxygen. With the rocket blazing, the X-15 climbed to the edge of the atmosphere, on the very fringes of space, where small jets in the nose and wings helped to keep it steady and on course. The X-15 made so many flights near to the edge of space that six of the 12 pilots qualified for astronaut's wings. Much of the technology that later went into making the Space Shuttle was tested on the X-15.

SPACE SHUTTLE

Tiled surface
On re-entry, friction between the orbiter and the Earth's atmosphere heats the outside of the craft to as much as 1,500 °C. Much of the orbiter's surface is covered by a protective layer of silica-fibre tiles, which fit together like the pieces of a jigsaw. The tiles absorb heat and prevent the orbiter from melting. The tip of the nose and the wings' leading edges get hottest, so they are also coated with a special type of carbon for extra heat insulation.

Flight deck
The pilot and mission commander sit on the flight deck. There are also two seats for specialist astronauts who may need to be on the flight deck during the mission.

Structure
The 37-metre- (100-foot-) long orbiter has a construction similar to a normal airplane, with a framework made of light aluminium alloy.

Space laboratory

Robot arm
Controlled from inside the orbiter, this long jointed arm can lift satellites out of the payload bay and recapture them in orbit.

Mid-deck
During the mission, which may last up to 16 days, the living area for the seven astronaut crew is the mid-deck. Some sleeping berths are horizontal and others are vertical, but it doesn't really matter in a weightless environment. There is also a washroom, a galley and an airlock allowing access into the unpressurized payload bay.

Windows
The heat-resistant, triple-glazed windows are 65 millimetres (2.5 inches) thick.

Thrusters
Small adjustments to the craft's orbit can be made by firing different combinations of the 44 jet thrusters.

Discovery

Lower deck
The crew's life-support systems are housed in the orbiter's lower deck. Air-filters remove carbon dioxide and water vapour breathed out by the astronauts, keeping the air breathable.

LAUNCHING THE SHUTTLE

The speed needed to get into orbit around the Earth is an astonishing 28,080 kph (17,410 mph). To achieve this, the Shuttle's three main engines need the help of two solid-fuel boosters. These five engines produce as much power as more than 140 Boeing 747 jumbo jets! At an altitude of 45–50 kilometres (around 30 miles), the boosters shut down and fall back to Earth, slowed by parachutes. They drop into the ocean, to be recovered and used again.

A fuel tank attached to the bottom of the orbiter carries liquid hydrogen and liquid oxygen for the main engines to burn. After eight minutes, and a height of about 110 kilometres (68 miles), the fuel tank is jettisoned and burns up in the atmosphere. Less than 10 minutes after blast-off, the craft is in orbit.

Rudder

As well as being used to control the orbiter on its glide in to land, the two-piece rudder splits apart vertically to act as a brake and slow the orbiter down.

REUSABLE SPACECRAFT

In the past, launching spacecraft by rocket was costly and wasteful, because the rocket could only be used once. The USA's Space Shuttle programme made space travel cheaper by devising a spacecraft that could be used again and again. The Shuttle comprises a craft called an orbiter, a pair of rocket boosters and a huge fuel tank. Only the fuel tank cannot be reused. The Shuttle takes off like a rocket using the boosters and fuel tank, goes into orbit around the Earth and then returns like an airplane, with the orbiter gliding in to land on a conventional runway.

The Shuttle can be used to launch space probes on their journeys to distant planets, set satellites on their orbits and retrieve them for repair. It can also hold a small space laboratory in its payload bay where scientists carry out experiments.

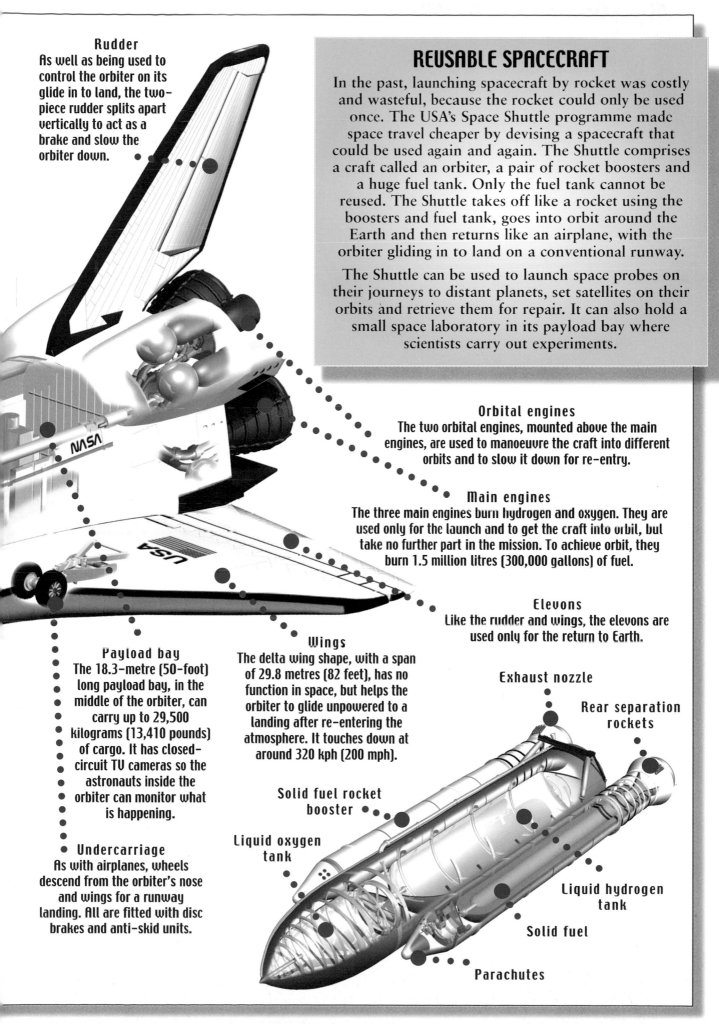

Orbital engines

The two orbital engines, mounted above the main engines, are used to manoeuvre the craft into different orbits and to slow it down for re-entry.

Main engines

The three main engines burn hydrogen and oxygen. They are used only for the launch and to get the craft into orbit, but take no further part in the mission. To achieve orbit, they burn 1.5 million litres (300,000 gallons) of fuel.

Elevons

Like the rudder and wings, the elevons are used only for the return to Earth.

Exhaust nozzle

Rear separation rockets

Payload bay

The 18.3-metre (50-foot) long payload bay, in the middle of the orbiter, can carry up to 29,500 kilograms (13,410 pounds) of cargo. It has closed-circuit TV cameras so the astronauts inside the orbiter can monitor what is happening.

Wings

The delta wing shape, with a span of 29.8 metres (82 feet), has no function in space, but helps the orbiter to glide unpowered to a landing after re-entering the atmosphere. It touches down at around 320 kph (200 mph).

Solid fuel rocket booster

Liquid oxygen tank

Liquid hydrogen tank

Undercarriage

As with airplanes, wheels descend from the orbiter's nose and wings for a runway landing. All are fitted with disc brakes and anti-skid units.

Solid fuel

Parachutes

Index